About the Book

In the far northern Canadian wilderness a mother whooping crane lays two eggs in her nest. One of the eggs will be removed from the nest to be hatched in captivity where the young chick can be protected from the dangers of the wild. The other chick will depend upon its parents for protection as it grows bigger and finally strong enough to join them in the 1,800-mile flight to their winter home in Texas.

Lorle Harris tells the story of the first year of a young whooper's life. The cranes must be constantly on the watch for bears, coyotes, eagles and hawks, ever ready to make a meal of an unwary chick. On their flight to their wintering grounds they must avoid hunters' guns. They must fight winds that can toss a bird about like an autumn leaf or sweep it into a powerline.

Kazue Mizumura's fine illustrations provide a vivid picture of this nearly extinct North American bird that has been fighting for survival so long.

BIOGRAPHY OF A
Whooping Crane

by Lorle Harris
illustrations by Kazue Mizumura

G.P. Putnam's Sons New York

The author wishes to thank Dr. Ray C. Erickson, Assistant Director for Endangered Wildlife Research, Patuxent Wildlife Research Center, Laurel, Maryland, for his kind assistance and advice.

Text copyright © 1977 by Lorle K. Harris
Illustrations copyright © 1977 by Kazue Mizumura
All rights reserved. Published
simultaneously in Canada by
Longman Canada Limited, Toronto.
PRINTED IN THE UNITED STATES OF AMERICA
07211
Library of Congress Cataloging in Publication Data
Harris, Lorle K
Biography of a whooping crane.
(Nature biography)
SUMMARY: Follows a year in the life of a family
of whooping cranes from their summer home in Canada
to their winter home in Texas.
1. Whooping cranes—Juvenile literature.
[1. Whooping cranes] I.Mizumura, Kazue. II. Title.
QL696.G84H37 1977   016.5983'1   76-23240
ISBN 0-399-20574-8
ISBN 0-399-61063-4 lib. bdg.

FOR BURTON

It was June. The last of the ice had disappeared from the network of ponds and lakes. Fresh green foliage softened the outlines of the tangled birch and willow thickets on the narrow ridges separating the ponds. Summer had returned to Wood Buffalo National Park in the northern Canadian wilderness.

Towering spruce stood black against the pale twilight sky. A firm mound of sedges and reeds, hidden among bulrushes and cattails, rose about a foot above the water. A whooping crane waited patiently to change places with her mate on the nest. He balanced himself gingerly, taking care not to disturb the eggs. When he stepped out, he stretched to his full height. He stood nearly five feet, only a little taller than the female.

The birds bent over to examine the two buff-colored eggs, twice the size of a hen's egg, that lay in the shallow nest. All was well.

Now the mother bird placed a foot on each side of the eggs. Twisting this way and that, she lowered herself into a setting position.

Once the eggs lay snug against her breast she scarcely moved. Only the wind whispering in the spruce tops broke the silence of the night. From time to time the crane stood up. She stretched her long neck to turn the eggs over gently with her beak.

Meanwhile, her mate patrolled the boundaries of the territory he claimed for his family. He held his head high and paused slightly at each step before lifting his foot. His satin-white plumage gleamed in the twilight.

He stepped behind the cattails. His mate saw only his red-capped head with its pointed black beak and the mustache of bristly black feathers that reached over his cheeks. His cold yellow eyes looked fierce as he scanned the area for wolves and lynx and the huge moose that could crush a crane's nest with one footstep.

Suddenly he sounded the alarm call: *Kerloo, ker-lee-oo!* He thrust his head and beak forward like a spear. Flapping his wings, he charged toward the far end of the pond. The bulrushes parted before him as he rushed to the water's edge.

A large black bear waded slowly through the water as he drank.

Kerloo, ker-lee-oo! The crane's giant steps barely skimmed the ground.

The bear looked up. He stared for a moment at the threatening beak, then lumbered off into the thicket. Breaking branches crunched under his feet.

The crane continued his patrol until it was time to relieve his mate on the nest.

The female stepped out. She took a round-about trail through the cattails to the shoreline to avoid calling attention to her nest. Not until she was a safe distance from the nest did she stop. She flapped her wings. Then she probed the mud for insect larvae.

A bald eagle, flying overhead, cast its shadow on the ground. The crane looked up, watching its flight. She returned to her feeding only after it had passed.

After about two hours the crane returned to the nest. She sat quietly for a long time. A song sparrow trilled in the brush. A red-winged blackbird flew across the pond. Then she heard a faint whirring sound overhead. It grew louder. The reflection of a helicopter moved across the water. The crane looked up.

Kerloo, ker-lee-oo! Her mate's cry mingled with her own.

She left the nest.

The helicopter dropped lower and disappeared behind tall spruce trees. The whirring of the motor stopped. For a time all was quiet. Then the crane heard the squish of footsteps sloshing through the bog.

A man stepped out of the brush and started toward the nest. The crane thrust her beak forward, ready to attack. She didn't frighten the man. He walked steadily toward the nest. She let her wing drop limply as if it were broken and stumbled into the brush.

Again and again her mate lowered his beak and thrust it toward the intruder. But the crane always kept a safe distance away. At last he, too, disappeared among the trees.

For several years now scientists had come to the wilderness while the whooping cranes were nesting. They removed one egg from the usual clutch of two, placed the egg in a woolen sock and carried it away.

It is unlikely that the cranes remembered what had happened to their clutch the year before. Nor did they know that the men placed the eggs in an incubator to hatch them and raise the chicks where they could be protected. In the wild it is rare for both chicks in a nest to grow up. Scientists have made sure that more of the young survive by hatching half of each year's eggs in captivity.

The cranes returned to the nest as soon as the man left. They examined the remaining egg. It was all right.

For thirty days the two birds had been taking turns brooding, sitting on the nest to hatch the eggs. Now the mother bird listened for the faint peeping that would tell her the chick was about to hatch. She rocked forward, stretching her neck under her breast to look at the egg. Sure enough, the egg had a tiny hole.

Using his eggtooth at the tip of his beak, the little chick tapped against the shell. All day and all night it piped and tapped. It stopped often to rest. At last it broke through the membrane and shell. The wet, downy chick pushed its way out of the shell. The tawny-colored bird was so weak it could hardly hold up its head.

It took about an hour for the tiny crane's coat to dry. Now her down was fluffy, and she could stand on her wobbly legs for a few minutes.

Before hatching both cranes sometimes left the nest for short periods. Now they brooded the chick almost constantly to keep it warm.

The mother dug a bristle worm out of the mud. She worked the food in her bill and tried to put it in the chick's bill. The chick turned away, and the mother swallowed the tidbit. The mother offered the chick another tidbit. Again the chick refused to eat. She was nearly a day old before she swallowed her first bit of food.

Not until the next day did the chick leave the nest. She walked a few feet, then returned to cuddle under her mother's wings.

Within a few days the chick was out of the nest most of the time. For about a week the cranes returned at night to bed down in the nest. The mother sat down in the middle, gathering the grass about her for bedding. The chick cuddled beneath her warm feathers while the father stood guard.

The mother awoke when the chick crawled out to drink some water. She watched her mate give the young one a mayfly. Only when the chick was safely under her wing again did she close her eyes.

The chick grew quickly. Soon she tripped after her parents as they strode through the mud, leaving broadly arrow-shaped footprints. She waded into the water when they went after diving beetles or water striders. She began to exercise her wings, even before her feathers were full-grown.

During this time her parents didn't fly as much as usual. They were shedding their feathers and replacing them with new ones. In whooping cranes this process happens every other year and is called molting.

One day great black clouds gathered on the horizon. Lightning zigzagged through the darkness, and thunder rumbled in the distance. A stiff wind blew ripples across the shallow water. It riffled the birds' feathers as they searched for snails on the mud.

The parent birds looked up often to watch their chick chasing mallard ducks along the shore. Her strides were growing longer every day, but she never caught a duck.

A frog jumped out of the bulrushes. The male crane stabbed it with one strike of his beak. He tore it up for the chick. She quickly gobbled it.

A white admiral butterfly darted in front of the chick. She chased it from bush to bush and into the thicket. Suddenly darkness surrounded her. She looked for an opening in the thick brush. Branches stabbed her whenever she moved. She piped constantly, calling her parents. She found an opening. Raindrops, hard as pebbles, struck her head. She ran headlong into her mother, tripping over the big crane's twig-like feet.

Kerloo, ker-lee-oo! her mother cried. She untangled the chick, forced her to her feet, and pushed her forward. The father bird hurried to his family.

Thunder crashed all about the birds. Lightning ripped through the clouds. Rain poured down on the cranes like water spilling over a dam. The father led his family to a tentlike shelter under the willows. The cranes shook the water from their feathers. They huddled together until the rain stopped.

The sky grew lighter. The birds stepped out of their hiding place. A shower of water slid off the leaves, drenching the cranes again. Once more they shook themselves dry.

One day the little crane chased a pair of ducklings halfway across the pond. When the water became too deep for wading, she returned to

the shore. She flopped down to rest at the water's edge.

Her mother looked all about to be sure the chick was in no danger. The adult bird continued feeding.

The ducks returned from across the pond and were now swimming only a short distance from the sleeping chick.

The mother crane snatched a minnow from the water and swallowed it. As she glanced again at her chick, a dark form swooped through the air with the speed of an arrow toward her youngster.

The mother rushed to attack the duck hawk, her beak thrust out like a sword. *Kerloo, ker-lee-oo!*

Her mate streaked toward the chick from the opposite direction. But it was a duckling the hawk had singled out as its prey. It landed on the duck's back, bit through its neck, and, clasping it firmly in its claws, turned upward and leaped into the air.

The chick opened her eyes and stretched. Her mother snapped at a damselfly and gave it to her. Her father returned to guard duty.

By September the young crane had grown from the newly hatched bird, half the size of a robin, to the height of a ten-year-old child. Rusty feathers now replaced most of the down that had covered the baby chick. As these feathers grew out, their white bases showed, giving the young crane a mottled appearance. She strayed farther from her parents now, but they never let her out of their sight.

Now the days were growing shorter. Darkness replaced the twilight of summer nights. Clouds of fog settled on the water during the night. Often a lacy border of ice crystals fringed the pond in the morning. As the sun rose in the sky, the fog and ice disappeared.

The whooping cranes grew restless. It was almost time for the long trip south. The parents had spent most of the summer caring for their chick. Now it was time to strengthen their wings for the long flight.

Stretching his neck and head forward and slightly downward, the male ran a few steps. He flapped his wings upward in short arcs, raising his body into the air. His wings unfolded gradually to their seven-foot span as he circled and wheeled to fly higher. He called his mate to join him.

And she did. She soared to a height many times higher than the treetops. The two birds circled and dipped while the young crane watched from the ground.

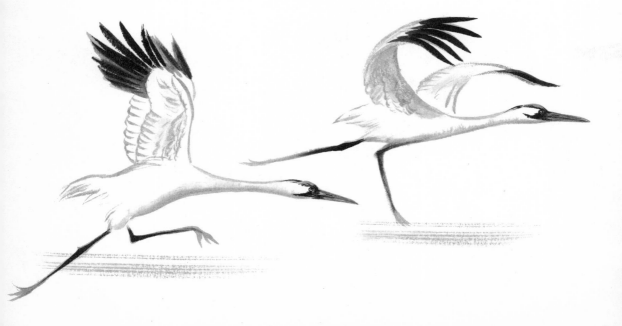

Soon she, too, felt the excitement of her parents. She ran about, flapping her wings, copying the big birds movements. Suddenly, she too, was airborne.

Her mother flew to her side. They flew a short distance together. Then the mother glided to the earth. She cupped her wings and braced her feet firmly as she touched the ground. The youngster's feet sprawled as she landed, but she wasn't hurt.

Every day the cranes practiced flying. Within ten days the young crane could fly several hundred yards. Not long afterward she joined her parents as they flew ever higher and farther from their territory. They passed over neighboring ponds. They watched the wood buffalo and moose grazing in the marshy meadows. They looked down on log-choked rivers. They saw the beaver dams and the partly finished lodges the beaver were building for the winter.

Once they met another whooping crane family soaring through the sky. They paid no attention to each other.

When they finished flying, the parent birds hunted more busily than ever for frogs and snails and midges and brought them to the chick. They gorged themselves, too. They were storing fat in their bodies for the long flight to their winter home in Texas. They would fly 2,500 miles to the Aransas National Wildlife Refuge on the shore of the Gulf of Mexico.

The days grew shorter. The thunder no longer rumbled overhead. Instead, the wind whistled more loudly in the treetops. Sometimes snowflakes swirled through the air. They settled on the ground and covered the fingers of ice that now stretched farther into the pond.

Still the birds waited and practiced flying. Not until the young crane could fly long distances without stopping could the birds begin their journey.

They chose a day when a strong wind swept down from the north. The male ran into the current. He whooped as the wind carried him upward and forward. His mate followed quickly, then the chick. The parents, whooping constantly, circled until the young bird flew between them.

Up and up the cranes flew so high the mountains, forests, and prairies flattened into irregular colored patches, so high they couldn't be seen from the ground. They traveled south through Canada, crossing the northeast corner of Alberta and cutting diagonally across Saskatchewan.

Route of Migration

When the small bird tired, her father scanned the ground for a stream. He flew closer to the ground, following the meandering lines until he found a sandbar. With wings widespread and his long black legs stretched behind, he slowly circled to the earth.

His family followed close behind. They fed
on grain in the nearby fields and roosted that
night in a sandbar in the middle of the stream.

When they awoke the next morning, a flight
of geese was flying overhead. Hundreds of birds
darkened the sky in great V-shaped clouds.

Suddenly a shot rang out and another and
another. Two geese tumbled out of the sky. A
hunting dog splashed into the water.

The parent birds cried out, *Kerloo, ker-lee-oo!*
They rose into the air, guarding the chick
between them.

A shot whizzed past. The mother bird looked anxiously at her chick. A pellet grazed the chick's wing. She teetered uncertainly, lost her balance and plunged downward.

Kerloo, ker-lee-oo! The parents dived after their young.

The chick flapped her wings frantically. She rose into the air, only to drop downward again. At last she regained her balance. Up and up she flew with strong, sure strokes. The cranes were safe.

Ever southward and eastward they flew. They stopped often to rest. A pair of whooping cranes without young passed them.

It was the middle of October when they reached the Platte River in Nebraska. The shrill *garooo-a-a-a, tuk-tuk, tuk-tuk, tuk-tuk* of the sandhill crane blended with the quacking and honking of ducks and geese as they landed. Nowhere else had they seen so many birds.

The cranes rested on the sandbars for several days. They flew over the nearby grainfields, where they caught unwary mice and grasshoppers. They gleaned the grain left by the reaping machines. Well fed and rested, they were ready to travel again.

Day after day they pressed onward. As the young crane grew stronger they covered greater distances—100, 125, even 150 miles a day.

Only stormy weather slowed the cranes' progress. Once hurricane winds from the gulf pelted them with raindrops. The birds beat their wings against the blasts, barely able to forge ahead, sometimes blown backward. A strong gust picked up the young crane and tossed her about like an autumn leaf.

Kerloo, ker-lee-oo! The adult birds wheeled about, letting the wind blow them to the youngster's side. They guided her downward to wait out the storm on the ground.

The wind carried them swiftly forward, too swiftly. It drove the male bird, headfirst, into a power line. Stunned by the blow, he bounced upward, then crashed to the ground.

His mate dived after him. *Kerloo, ker-lee-oo!* The young crane followed. They landed beside the fallen bird. He didn't move. His neck was strangely bent. The female touched him gently with her beak. She paced back and forth beside her mate. The chick imitated her mother's every move. All day and all night they watched over the big bird. Once more the female nudged her mate with her beak. It was no use; they would have to fly on without him.

The cranes flew until they saw the Gulf of Mexico stretching endlessly before them. Soon the older bird saw the familiar outline of the Blackjack Peninsula.

She circled over the salt flats where she and her mate had lived the past winter. The 400-acre site was dotted with little pools that swarmed with marine life. Receding tides trapped small fish and the whooping crane's favorite food, the blue crab, in the pools.

After several weeks the long journey was over. The mother glided to the water and probed for crabs. When she found one, she broke it up for the youngster.

Suddenly the piercing, shrill cry of a male whooping crane told them they were feeding on his territory. He thrust his beak forward and rushed toward them. His mate ran beside him. Her trumpeting mingled with his bugling in a frightening warning.

Mother and chick backed away. The angry pair chased them until they took to the air. They flew from one end of the peninsula to the other. Crane families had already found the best places. Without a mate to defend her homesite, the mother bird knew it was useless to settle here.

All winter long the cranes wandered through-out the Aransas Refuge. The trumpeting battle cries and the charging saberlike beaks of the paired birds forced them away from the best feeding places.

They were not the only cranes without a terri-tory of their own. Older birds without mates and young ones, not yet paired, also wandered about in search of food. Sometimes these cranes formed little groups of their own, but they never chased the mother and her chick away.

When winter winds flooded the feeding places near the shore, the cranes fled to higher ground. They ate the acorns they found in groves of oak trees. They fed on grain put out by the refuge staff.

At night they roosted on sandbars in the center of shallow ponds. The young crane huddled close to her mother when a coyote howled in the dark.

One day the birds were feeding near a clump of mesquite bushes. A large snake sunned himself on a bare patch of ground nearby. The older crane paid no attention. The chick began to pipe and dance.

Whir . . . whir. . . . The snake rattled a warning.

The young crane flapped her wings. She pranced toward the snake.

The mother bird leaped on the snake. Her beak struck at him, pinning his head to the ground. She stabbed the snake again and again, then swallowed him whole.

Winter was nearly over. The young crane lost most of the cinnamon-colored feathers that had covered her since she had lost her downy coat. Her new feathers gleamed satin-white like her mother's, and she stood nearly as tall. The two cranes were no longer chased from the territories of other birds so often. They fed quietly while the birds soared in the air, testing their wings for the spring migration.

Sometimes a crane pumped his head up and down as if bowing to his mate. Mother and chick felt the excitement of their kind getting ready for another mating and the flight to the north.

One day a large male walked toward the mother bird. He bowed his head. He flapped his wings. Then, holding his legs stiff, jumped straight up into the air. He leaped nearly eight feet off the ground. His wings flapped constantly, showing the fringe of black flight feathers. He arched his head and neck over his back. His beak pointed toward the sky.

The female ran to the crane as he touched the ground. She flapped her wings and pumped her head up and down. Then both cranes jumped together. They landed on stiff legs. Like balls, the birds bounced into the air again. The female bowed her head as she came down, and the male leaped over her bent back.

The young crane tried clumsily to imitate her mother. The adult birds ignored her.

After the dance the cranes stopped to preen. The female waded into the water. She crouched so low all but her neck and head was covered. She splashed about, flapping her wings and wiggling her tail. Then she stood up, shook herself, flapped her wings, and drew her beak through her feathers.

She began feeding again. The young crane ran to her. She pecked in the mud at her mother's feet, waiting impatiently for a tidbit. With a quick thrust, the mother turned her sharp bill on the chick. She backed away in surprise. Again and again her mother chased her away. At last the young crane understood. She would have to find her own food now.

After that the adult pair danced almost every day. And every day the young crane found her own dinner.

The days grew longer and warmer. One day early in April a steady, soft wind blew from the south. The male crane took off into the wind. His new mate and her young followed close behind. Up and up they spiraled, whooping constantly. Soon they could no longer see the wintering grounds.

When the cranes reached southern Canada, the young crane left her parents. Whether she would spend the summer alone or with other young cranes, no one knows for certain, but she would return to the Aransas Refuge in the fall. Not until she is five or six years old will she have young of her own, although she may select a mate earlier.

The mother and her new mate returned to Wood Buffalo National Park. A new year had begun.

AUTHOR'S NOTE

Once large flocks of whooping cranes, *Grus americana,* lived in the central regions of North America. By 1938 only fifteen wild cranes remained.

Wildlife conservationists wanted to help the whooping cranes survive. To do so, they needed to protect the birds on migration and in their nesting grounds as well as in their winter home, the Aransas National Wildlife Refuge in Texas. Their nesting grounds were in the far north, exactly where, no one knew.

After a five-year search American and Canadian naturalists found the nesting site in Wood Buffalo National Park. Now they could protect the birds wherever they were.

The whooping crane flock grew very slowly. So many dangers faced the newborn chicks that only one out of four reached Texas. Scientists tried an experiment. Since the cranes laid two eggs in a setting, why not take one egg from each nest and raise the chick in captivity? This was tried, and it worked.

By 1974 there were fifty wild cranes and seventeen captive birds at the Patuxent Wildlife Research Center in Maryland.

But scientists worried that a single bad storm might wipe out the entire wild flock. Why not start a second flock in a different place, one that followed a different migration route?

In 1975 scientists placed whooping crane eggs in the nests of the closely related sandhill cranes living in Idaho. The sandhill cranes accepted the strange eggs. The young followed their foster parents to their wintering grounds in New Mexico.

The future of the whoopers is still in doubt, but it looks very hopeful.

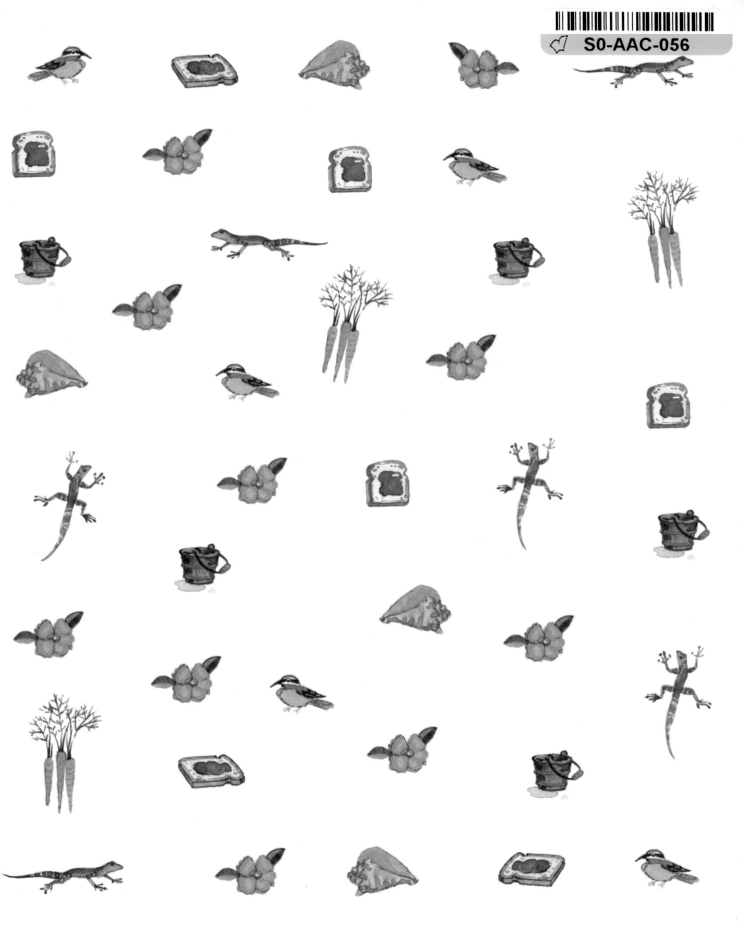

Satchi
and
Little Star

By Donna Marie Seim

Illustrated by Susan Spellman

*To Gracie
Big hugs from
Satchi and
Little Star
♡
Donna Seim*

Jetty House

An imprint of Peter E. Randall Publisher
Portsmouth, NH
2011

Dedication

To all the beautiful wild horses in the world! And in particular, to the wild horses on Grand Turk—they are the inspiration for this story.

To Martin, my husband and best friend, who believes in me and supports all of my writing endeavors. And to Kristin, my daughter, who encouraged me to write down my stories!

A portion of the proceeds from this book will be donated to the TCSPCA—Grand Turk Chapter of the Turks and Caicos Islands.

First Edition 2011

Published by Jetty House
An imprint of Peter E. Randall Publisher
Box 4726, Portsmouth, NH 03802-4726
www.perpublisher.com

(ISBN 13) 978–0–9828236–7–5
(ISBN 10) 0–9828236–7–3

Library of Congress Control Number: 2011932957

The story of Satchi, an island girl, who tries to catch and tame a wild horse.

Visit http://www.donnaseim.com to learn more about Donna's books.

Printed in Canada

Book design and color separations by Ed Stevens, www.edstevensdesign.com

Author's Note

Can you imagine finding a handsome herd of eight wild horses lined up at your gate waiting patiently for you to let them in? On Grand Turk in the Turks and Caicos Islands, you can experience this very scene! Small herds of wild horses roam free there. The houses are surrounded by stone walls, each sporting a colorful gate, to protect the tasty grass and gardens within. If you don't like to mow your lawn, just leave your gate open—the horses will keep the grass well clipped!

The first time I laid eyes on a wild horse, I fell in love, and just like Satchi I daydreamed about taming my very own horse. An island friend told me it was easy: just feed them some jelly bread, and soon you will have yourself a horse! But it is not quite so simple, as Satchi finds out!

Wild horses are descendants of domesticated horses, but they are smaller due to their lean diets. They live on grasses and need fresh water to survive. If they are lucky, they can drink from fresh water springs or wells. They also forage for rainwater and are even resourceful enough to dig their own wells, using their hooves as shovels!

How did wild horses come to live on islands? Their ancestors may have been brought by early settlers, or they may have been survivors from shipwrecks. Either way, the horses were left behind to fend for themselves. They became wild, using their natural instincts for survival.

Harsh climates and lack of fresh water have brought wild horses close to extinction on some islands. They are now protected in many areas, considered national treasures to be enjoyed and appreciated for the graceful, gorgeous creatures they are.

Wild horses live around the world on islands, in forests, on the plains and in the mountains. To name just a few, there are the Chincoteague wild ponies on Assateague Island, the Bankers on the outer banks of North Carolina, the Abaco wild horses of the Bahamas, the Australian Brumby, the Misaki ponies of Japan, the protected Mustangs of the American West, and the handsome wild horses that roam free on many Caribbean islands, including the Turks and Caicos.

Satchi hopped out of her papa's truck singing, "I am Satchi, island girl!
I will open the gate!" A herd of eight wild horses trotted past.

The littlest one had a white star on his forehead and one white sock.
Satchi loved his brown furry coat and buttery-colored mane.
She yearned to stroke his nose!

4

That afternoon, Satchi asked her mama, "May I have a horse for my very own?"

"Horses cost lots of money and eat lots of hay," her mother said, bouncing Satchi's baby brother on her knee.

"But Mama, the wild horses are free and they eat grass."

"Satchi, wild horses are meant to be wild!"

The next day Satchi went to the gate and waited for the horses.
A hummingbird *zum-zumm*ed above her head. She heard
the clomp, clomp of horse's hooves. The herd of eight
horses pranced by.

Satchi sang out, "Oh, little one with the white star,
I am Satchi, island girl! I will be your friend!
If I could tame you, I would name you Little Star!"

Satchi ran to ask her papa, "Can we drive to the creek to watch the wild horses drink?"

"Why don't you play with your brother instead?"

"But Papa, there is a little horse with a white star. I could tame him for my very own."

"Satchi! Wild horses are meant to be wild."

Satchi tried not to think about Little Star, but she couldn't forget his big brown eyes or his one white sock.

"Well, if Mama won't say yes, and if Papa won't help,
I will tame Little Star by myself. If I bring water to the gate,
Little Star will not have to walk all the way to the creek
to drink. Then he will know I am his friend!"

Satchi filled a bucket with water and sloshed a wet trail to the gate. A lizard sat on the gate watching her.

She heard horses neighing.

The horses and Little Star pranced on by.

None of them stopped to sniff at her bucket of cool water. Satchi chanted, "Tomorrow, Little Star, tomorrow I will bring you crunchy carrots."

The next day Satchi carried two carrots and a bucket of water to the gate. A mockingbird chirped at her. She heard the sound of horse's hooves.

"Oh, Little Star! I am Satchi, island girl! I am your friend." Little Star's eyes met hers, but he did not stop. Satchi sang, "Tomorrow, Little Star, tomorrow I will bring you sweet jelly bread!"

At lunchtime Satchi saved her jelly bread. She skipped down to the gate. The stallion trotted by holding his head high. Little Star was last in line. Satchi cooed, "Little Star! I am Satchi, island girl. I am your friend."

Little Star stepped forward, sniffing the sweet jelly. His nose tickled Satchi's hand. Then, as quick as quick could be, the jelly bread was gone!

"Little Star, I will bring you jelly bread every day. Now we are friends!"

Satchi met Little Star every day for a whole week.
She stroked his nose and petted his furry mane.
She fed him jelly bread and cooed to him,
"Little Star, I am Satchi, island girl. You are my friend!"

One afternoon Satchi found a rope in the shed and tied a loop with a knot. Then she climbed up on the gate to wait. Little Star pranced toward her. Satchi offered him the jelly bread. Little Star whinnied and took the bread. Satchi, as quick as quick could be, slipped the rope over his head.

Little Star pulled away, but she held on tight. He rose up on his hind legs with his front hooves pawing the air. Satchi was frightened. She dropped the rope. Little Star ran away with the rope trailing behind him.

18

Satchi was quiet that night. Papa asked her why she was not full of stories, and Mama felt her forehead. Satchi went to bed early. All she could think about was Little Star.

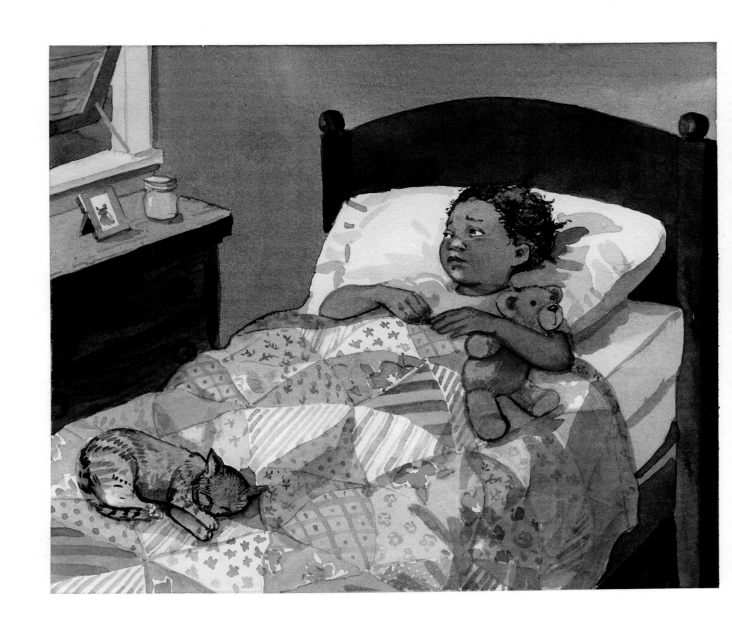

The next morning, Satchi sat on the gate. The sun was hot and there was no wind. When the parade of horses approached, her eyes searched for Little Star. "Oh no! There are only seven horses!" she cried, "Little Star is missing!"

She walked down the dusty road that led
to where the thickest thorn bushes grew.

She called into the thorny thicket,
"Little Star! It is me, Satchi, island girl. I have jelly bread!"
The only answer she heard was the shrill cry of an osprey.

Satchi sat down on a stump of a tree.
Tears dribbled down her cheeks.
"I must find Little Star!"

Satchi followed a path that wound around the thorny briars.
Prickers pulled at her skirt and scratched her legs. She sobbed,
"Little Star! Satchi is coming!"

In the deepest thicket Satchi found Little Star. His rope was laced around a bush full of thorns as sharp as needles. He had many scratches and a cut on his white sock. Satchi cooed and raised the jelly bread to his mouth. Little Star was hungry!

Satchi found the end of the rope. She yanked out the sharp thorns until the rope was free. "Come Little Star. I am Satchi, island girl. I am your friend. We will go home and clean your cuts."

Satchi led him to the shed. She slipped the rope off of his neck. Then she cleaned him with warm soap and water. Papa put salve on his cuts and Mama wound a bandage around his leg. Little Star drank from the pail of water and then he lay down on the cool dirt floor. Satchi stroked his nose and said, "Good night, Little Star, sleep tight."

She closed the door to the shed and walked back to the house. Her mama was waiting to tuck her into her cozy quilt. As Satchi snuggled into her bed, she wondered if Little Star would be lonely out in the shed, but she was so tired she couldn't keep her eyes open any longer.

Early the next morning, Satchi awoke to loud neighing. She hurried to the shed and swung open the door. Little Star bolted past her and galloped to the gate. Satchi ran after him, calling, "Little Star! Come back! I will feed you carrots and jelly bread!"

There, on the other side of the gate, stood the stallion and the herd of horses. Satchi knew what she must do. She reached up and unlatched the gate. Little Star kicked up his heels and ran to join his herd. He whinnied and shook his head. Then he looked back at Satchi with his big brown eyes.

Satchi waved and called out to him,
  "Oh, Little Star, wild horses are meant to be free!
    I am Satchi, island girl. I will always be your friend!"

Fun Facts about Horses

A baby horse is called a foal. It drinks its mother's milk for its first six months. By age two, a horse is grown up.

A full grown female is called a mare and the male is called a stallion. There is only one stallion in a herd; young stallions, or bachelors, will create new herds.

Wild horses are herd animals and live in groups. Herds range in size from as few as three horses to as many as twelve or more.

Horses' ears point forward when they are alert and happy. Tense, laid back ears mean they are nervous or afraid. Relaxed ears mean they are bored or sleepy.

Horses communicate by neighing or whinnying. They have excellent hearing and a keen sense of smell. They also have clear vision and very strong teeth.

Horses need very little sleep; they can sleep standing up. Every few days, though, they will lie down and sleep for short periods. In a wild herd, several horses will stand on guard while others rest.

A white patch on a horse's forehead is called a star. A white patch above the hoof is called a sock. A large white patch on the face is called a blaze, and a narrow strip of white down the face is called a race.

Wild horses will run away if they are afraid or threatened. They will bite or kick with their hooves if they think you are a predator, but they are naturally curious animals and show interest in people who are friendly.

About the Author

Donna Seim

Satchi and Little Star is the story of an island girl who tries to catch and tame a wild horse for her very own. Inspiration for this story is from Donna's love of wild horses.

Where is Simon, Sandy? Donna's first picture book is an award winning story, based on a true tale, about a little donkey that wouldn't quit.

Hurricane Mia is her first novel for eight to twelve year olds, an exciting adventure story set in the Caribbean!

A graduate of the Ohio State University, Donna also holds a masters degree in special education from Lesley University.

When Donna is not in the Caribbean, she lives in Newbury, Massachusetts, with her husband, Martin, and her dog, Rags.

You can visit Donna at www.donnaseim.com.

About the Illustrator

Susan Spellman

Susan has a studio workshop in Newburyport, Massachusetts, where she pursues a dual career as a fine artist and as an illustrator with extensive experience in painting, portraiture, and children's book illustration.

Susan has illustrated previous books by Donna Seim, such as *Where is Simon, Sandy?* and *Hurricane Mia*. In addition to many other books, including *Pinky and Bubs' Stinky Night Out* and just recently *Oscar the Herring Gull,* she has illustrated stories for children's magazines and for anthologies such as *A Treasury of Christmas Tales* and *A Treasury of Bedtime Stories.*

Susan also creates paintings and exhibits regularly in the New England area and is a member of The Newburyport Ten plein air painters, the Women in the Wild, and the Newburyport Art Association.

Her illustration work can be viewed at: www.suespellmanstudio.com and her fine art at www.spellmancollection.com